doll Crafts

Make your doll accessories to fill her world!

⭐ American Girl®

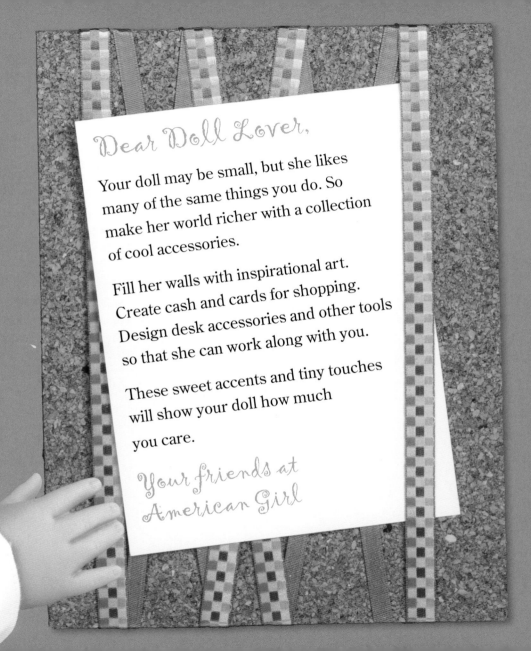

Dear Doll Lover,

Your doll may be small, but she likes
many of the same things you do. So
make her world richer with a collection
of cool accessories.

Fill her walls with inspirational art.
Create cash and cards for shopping.
Design desk accessories and other tools
so that she can work along with you.

These sweet accents and tiny touches
will show your doll how much
you care.

Your friends at
American Girl

Getting Started

Adult's Help

If the directions read 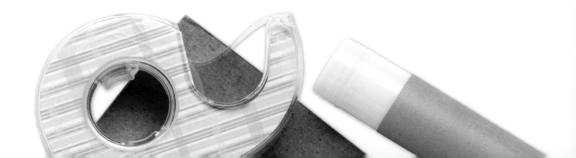 "Ask an adult to help," *always* check with an adult before working any further. Ask an adult to help you cut thick cardboard or foam core. A parent will also need to help you hang the posters, mirror, calendar, and clock on your doll's walls, because you might need pushpins, tacks, or tape.

Create Copies

Tip: Before you fold, glue, or tape any paper objects, make color copies so that you can make more!

Punch It Out

Punch out the pieces you'll need before starting a craft. *Be very careful when punching out the projects or they could tear!*

Choose a Cardboard

When picking a cardboard to use in your projects, think about how thick you want your cardboard to be. If you want the board to be really thick, use corrugated cardboard or foam core. Foam core is similar to cardboard, but it has a soft, thick middle.

Sticking Stuff

If the directions read, "Tape together," look at the project and decide whether it needs a strong tape, like packing tape, or a lightweight adhesive tape. A glue stick also works well for most of these projects.

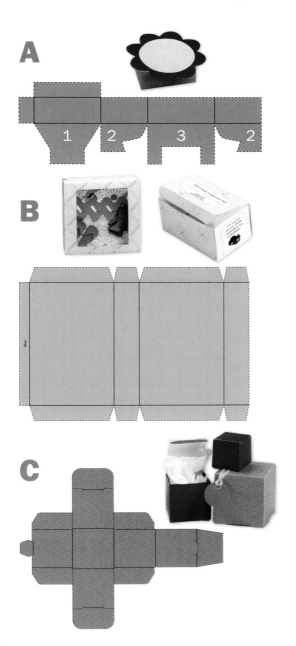

A

1   2   3   2

B

Glue

C

Folding Facts

Most of the craft boxes in your kit will fold naturally along the fold lines.

The boxes shown at left are the *basic* boxes in your kit—although they will have slight variations. For instance, we've added a flap to template B to make a shoulder bag and have removed the center panel for a shadow box.

For boxes shaped like A, glue the sides together first, and then fold the bottom flaps in the numbered order shown. Tuck in the number 3 flap. Glue the box lid to the top flap.

For boxes shaped like B, be sure to spread a little glue on the front and back flaps marked "Glue" before closing.

For the boxes shaped like C, fold closed by slipping the tabs in place—no gluing needed!

Take a Message

Show you care—even when you're not there—with memos and photos.

Bulletin Board

Create a place to stick nice notes and friendly photos for your doll. To start, pull out the bulletin board from your kit. Tape down one end of a pretty ribbon in back with packing tape, position the ribbon on the front where you want it, and then tape the other end in back. Repeat with more ribbons. Slip lightweight items between the ribbons.

Tip: Use adhesive tape to tape down your ribbons so that you can adjust them. Add the packing tape afterward.

See you soon!
Love,
Emma

Notepad

To leave your doll a quick note, write her a message on the mini notepad in your kit.

Mandy's
B-day
Saturday!

Room Mirror

Every doll needs a mirror for quick hair checks. To make one, glue the reflective plastic sheet from your kit on top of the corrugated cardboard from your kit. If you'd like, trim the mirror with pretty ribbons and flowers. Be sure to hang the mirror at your doll's eye level.

Deck the Walls

Spice up your doll's space with creativity and color.

Wall Clock

Craft a darling clock for your doll. To make one, glue the clock face from your kit to a 3½-inch square cardboard box lid. Cut 2 craft foam strips for hands.  With an adult's help, use a pushpin to poke a hole in the center of the lid and a hole in the bottom edge of each foam clock hand. Slip a brad through the holes and through the lid. Open the brad in back. Hang the clock at your doll's height.

Tip: A scrapbooking brad will be too short for this craft. Be sure to use a regular one!

Mood Posters

Give your doll's place a modern look with graphic posters. Punch out the posters from your kit and hang them on your doll's walls.

Come to Order

Organize your doll's life with these three tools.

Planner

Delight your doll with a planner. To make it, punch out the planner cover from your kit. Lay the cover on a piece of cardboard, and trace around it. Cut out the cardboard, and glue the cover to it. Place the planner in your doll's backpack or purse.

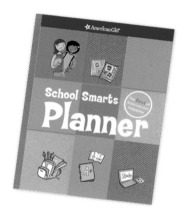

Wastebasket

Take out the trash with a doll-sized designer wastebasket. Punch out the wrap from your kit, and glue or tape it around a tiny disposable cup. Fill up the can with scrap paper!

Calendar

Keep track of your doll's holidays, important dates, and birthdays!

1 Stack the calendar pages from your kit—marked A through G—on top of one another in the order shown, with the tab letters facing up.

2 Fold the stack of pages in half in the center. The cover of the calendar should now be on top. Run your fingernail down the folded edge to help the pages lie flat.

3 Open the folded stack. Staple along the center line. Cut off the tabs. Hang the calendar at your doll's height.

Shadow Boxes

Help your doll celebrate her memories with sweet shadow boxes. Fold together both the boxes in your kit, following the instructions for box B from page 5—but don't glue them together yet! Lay the two boxes on top of paper and trace around them. Cut out both papers and decorate them with sand, pretty cutouts, stickers, and small objects. Glue the decorated paper inside each shadow box, and then glue the boxes closed. Set the boxes out for your doll's guests to admire.

Make Memories

Create events and travels for your doll to look back on and smile.

Postcards

Just saying "Hi!" Punch out the postcards from your kit and write messages on the back to reveal how your doll enjoyed her "travels."

Picture Frames

Frame your doll's favorite photos in pretty picture holders. To make them, pull out the frames from your kit, and then pop out the stand on the back of each one. Fold each frame in half, and slide in a photo. Glue down the sides. Stand frames on a shelf or table.

13

Picture This!

Pets, pals, parents—document your doll's world with photos.

Friendly Photos

Cut out your doll's friends and favorite pets from doll catalogues or magazines. To stiffen the photos, glue them to pieces of cardboard. Slip the pictures into photo holders. Be sure to add your own school photo to the mix!

Mod Photo Holders

Make hip clip holders for your doll's loose photos, postcards, or notes. Slip the items into large and small binder clips. Arrange the clips on a desk, dresser, or tabletop.

Set the Table

Turn your doll's table into a delightful place to dine.

Vase

Show off your doll's great taste with a colorful vase. To make one, tightly wrap the vase paper from your kit around a small thread spool, and then tape the vase closed. For a base, glue a foam circle on the bottom for the spool to rest on.

Dinner Napkins

Don't forget the napkins! For each napkin, cut a tiny square on the fold of a paper napkin from your kit. Stack, fold, or arrange the napkins on your doll's table.

"Fresh" Flowers

Brighten your doll's table with a bouquet of flowers. Punch out the flowers from your kit. Glue a flower front and matching back over a thin green chenille stem. Repeat with other flowers and leaves. Arrange the flowers in your doll's vase, and place the vase on the table.

Table Runner

Add interest to your doll's table with a runner. To design one, place 2 of the napkins from your kit side by side. Tape them together. On the opposite side, cover the seam (where the napkins touch) with a strip of ribbon and two-sided tape. Add more ribbon to decorate. Lay the runner along the center of the table.

Take a Break

Give your doll time off from homework for a little recreation.

Art Supplies

Keep supplies handy for your doll's creative days. To make an art pad, wrap the cover from your kit over a piece of corrugated cardboard from your kit, and glue the cover down. For a paintbrush, have an adult press both tips of a toothpick against a hard work surface to break off the ends. Color the paintbrush with markers.

Jump Rope

Make your doll her own jump rope by taping the ends of 3 long pieces of embroidery floss to a work surface and braiding them into a rope. For handles, have an adult help you use a toothpick to put glue inside 2 matching beads, and then slip each end of the braid into a bead. Let dry.

Library Books

Start a little library for your doll. For each book, lay a cover from your kit onto cardboard and trace around it. Cut out the cardboard, and then glue the cover on top of it. Stack the books on your doll's desk or slip them into her book bag.

Checkers

Invite another doll over to play a game with your doll. For checkers, lay a checkerboard from your kit onto cardboard and trace around it. Cut out the cardboard and glue the checkerboard on top. For checkers, punch out 12 red and 12 black paper pieces, using the paper in your kit. Keep the game pieces together in a small bag.

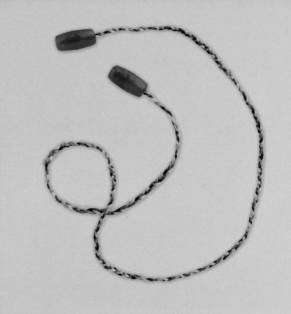

to be different!

✦ American Girl®

20

Look On My Desk

Your doll will find success with these cool desk tools.

Blotter

Pad your doll's desk like a professional's. Simply fold the blotter from your kit along fold lines and glue the flaps to seal it. Place the blotter to protect your doll's desktop.

Tissue Box

It's important to keep tissues nearby—especially during flu season! To make a box of them, fold together the box from your kit, following the instructions for box C on page 5. Cut off a 3-inch square from a regular tissue, and then push the tissue corner through the slot and into the box, leaving a little showing. Set the box on your doll's desk for sudden sneezes.

File Folders

Every desk has folders to file, so give your doll a set. To make them, fold the file folders from your kit in half, making sure the tabs stick above the files. Place a label sticker from the kit's sticker page onto each tab. Now file your doll's papers and documents, such as her birth certificate and report cards.

Pencil Cup and Pencil

A sharp pencil makes a sharp mind! To give your doll a pencil and a place to put it, glue the pencil-cup paper from your kit to a pump spray bottle cap. Trim paper, if needed. Then ask an adult to help you wrap and glue the kit's pencil paper around a toothpick. Color the toothpick end with a black marker. Place the cup within easy reach.

Learn to Relax

Give your doll ways to relax after a busy day.

Yoga Mat

Create a mat for your doll to carry to class. To start, cut a rectangle of fun foam and roll it as shown. Run glue along the long edge and press and hold until it sticks. Let dry. For a strap, trim a piece of ribbon to the proper length so that she can sling the mat over her shoulder. Glue the ribbon as shown at right. Or skip the glue and leave the mat flat!

Wrap and glue a long ribbon around one side.

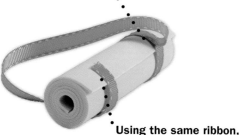

Using the same ribbon, repeat on the other side.

Chamomile Tea

When your doll can't sleep, help her relax with chamomile tea. To make the tea box from your kit, fold it, following the instructions for box B on page 5. Decorate the box using the sweet labels from the sticker sheet in your kit.

Boom Box

Your doll will be ready to rock with her very own boom box! Fold the boom box from your kit, following the instructions for box B on page 5. Glue on the handle as shown.

Relaxation CD

Every CD collection needs a soothing single. To make your doll one, punch out the CD cover from your kit. Fold the flaps, run a tiny line of glue on them, and then fold the cover over so that the flaps are inside. Let dry. Punch out the CD and slip it into the case.

Shoulder Bag

If your on-the-go doll needs a bag, this one should do the trick! To make it, punch out the bag and the 2 decorative flowers from your kit. Fold the bag, following the instructions for box B on page 5. Glue the flowers together as shown, and then glue them to the bag flap. For a strap, punch a hole on each side of the bag as marked. Tightly curl the ends of a long ribbon, push them through the holes on each end of the bag, and then knot the ends. Fill the bag with a wallet and other accessories.

Make Money

Give your doll a little independence with these cash-and-carry crafts.

Wallet and Cash

To offer your doll her own cash, punch out the wallet from your kit. Fold and glue as shown on the wallet. Let dry. Punch out the doll dollars, and then slip them inside the wallet.

Important Cards

Now your doll can use her own cards when visiting the places you go. Punch out the bus pass, library card, and gift card from your kit. Be sure to sign your doll's library card. The gift card has a $25 play value. And the bus pass is good for a lifetime. Slip the cards inside her wallet.

Pick a Card

Create cards for your doll to give and receive—any time of the year!

Greeting Cards

Special days can sneak up on your doll, so create a collection of cards she'll be able to use any time of the year. Punch out the cards from your kit and fold them in half. Choose a sticker for each card from the sticker sheet in your kit. Press the sticker on the front of the card. Help your doll write a message inside.

Envelopes

Add that special touch by creating an envelope for each card. Punch out the envelopes from your kit. Fold each one along the fold lines. Run glue along the flaps where shown, and then fold the envelope so that the flaps are inside. Address the envelope on the front. Slip in a card. Use the mini stamps from the sticker page.

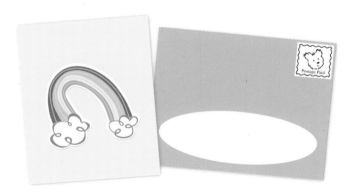

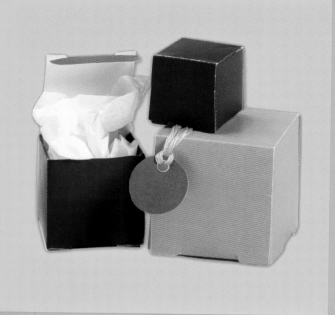

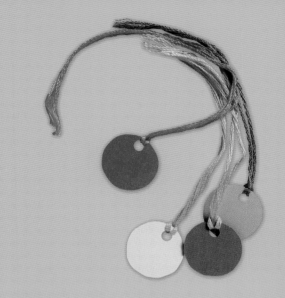

Personalize a Gift

Surprise your doll with lots of packages to give and get.

Gift Boxes

Sometimes the packaging can be as impressive as the gift! To help your doll give a gift that shines, punch and fold each gift box, following the instructions for box C on page 5. If you wish, add a mini bow and a gift tag.

Gift Tags

Make sure the person receiving a gift from your doll knows it came from her! To attach a tag, slip a strand of floss into the small hole in the gift tag and tape the floss to the box. On the gift tag, write who the gift is for and who it's from.

Beauty Boxes

Your doll's special days will require special packages. When such a day comes, be ready with an extra-special box. To make one, punch out the beauty box and lid from your kit. Fold the box, following the instructions for box A on page 5, and glue the lid to the flap.

Gift Wrap

Wrap gifts that really impress with pretty paper. Before you begin, slip a small gift (or a rock!) into the gift box to give it weight. (This will make wrapping easier.) Then pull out the wrapping paper from your kit and help your doll tape it on. Add a bow and a gift tag to finish.

Love doll
crafts?

Did you enjoy this book? Let us know! Write to:

Doll Crafts Editor
American Girl
8400 Fairway Place
Middleton, WI 53562

**(Photos can't be returned. All comments and suggestions received by
American Girl may be used without compensation or acknowledgment.)**

Published by American Girl Publishing, Inc.
Copyright © 2008 by American Girl, LLC

Questions or comments? Call 1-800-845-0005, visit our Web site at **americangirl.com**,
or write to Customer Service, American Girl, 8400 Fairway Place, Middleton, WI 53562-0497.

Printed in China
08 09 10 11 12 13 LEO 10 9 8 7 6 5 4 3

All American Girl marks are trademarks of American Girl, LLC.

Editorial Development: Trula Magruder, Camela Decaire; Art Direction & Design: Camela Decaire; Production: Jeannette Bailey, Gretchen Krause,
Judith Lary, Mindy Rappe, Kendra Schluter; Photography: Radlund Studios; Stylists: Camela Decaire, Carrie Anton, Mandy Crary

Here are some other American Girl books you might like:

❏ *I read it.*

❏ *I read it.*

❏ *I read it.*

❏ *I read it.*